CHAPTER 1

INTRODUCTION

Belly dancers are often used in Europe and America as symbols of a sensuous and exotic Orient. They appear in Orientalist paintings, novels by Flaubert and Colette, the legends of Little Egypt and Mata Hari, movies directed by Cecil B. De Mille, and even Disney cartoons. We see interpretations of the dance in performances of <u>Salome</u> and <u>The Nutcracker</u>, Middle Eastern and Greek restaurants, and Renaissance Festivals--almost invariably featuring scantily clad young women performing for male enjoyment. While we tend to assume that these portrayals accurately reflect the dance as it is practiced in the lands of its origin, they actually perpetuate a number of erroneous stereotypes:

The belly dance is a rather anachronistic dance of the harem.
It is a dance of seduction.
It is only performed by women for men.
Only young women perform the dance.
The dance has no culturally sanctioned role within the modern Middle East.

All of these stereotypes are at least partially incorrect. In reality, belly dancing plays an integral role in both westernized and traditional Middle Eastern women's lives, in which--according to anthropologist Karin Van Nieuwkerk, who has done extensive fieldwork with professional belly dancers in Cairo--"singing and dancing are essentially regarded as expressions of rejoicing" (1).

The etymology of the words for dance in Arabic (*raks*) and Turkish (*rakkase*) point to this aspect of dancing as well. Both are derived from the Assyrian word *radaku,* which means "to celebrate" (Buonaventura 60). Women of all ages (and--in certain situations--men) have performed versions of the belly dance since well before the advent of Islam (Zuhur, Images of Enchantment 6). As Van Nieuwkerk explains, "entertainers are central to the most important occasions in people's lives, such as births, engagements, and weddings. A celebration without performers is not a real celebration" (2).

There are several theories about belly dancing's origin, development, and dissemination. Dance historian Curt Sachs believes the dance was well-established as a performance art as far back as the Neolithic period (217). Moroccan scholar Fatima Mernissi writes that it began as a sacred ritual in temple ceremonies that honored Ishtar, the Semitic goddess of love (Scheherazade 70). Wendy Buonaventura traces stylistic elements of modern belly dancing from India, Persia, Arabia, Turkey, Morocco, Syria, Rome, Egypt, and Phoenicia; she offers linguistic evidence that suggests the dance may have been spread by the Romany people in their travels (41-44). Helland points out that the traditional geographical distribution of the belly dance is roughly that of the early Islamic crusades. Both Islam and belly dancing moved north to India, west to Spain, south to Africa, and east to Java (128).

The dance is used today for childbirth training and rituals, weddings, celebrations, women's private gatherings, and as entertainment. Women throughout the Middle East and North Africa learn belly dancing "as naturally as the ability to walk, watching their mothers, sisters and aunts" (Brooks 219). The dance is so ubiquitous that--to some--it is not even considered "art." Anthropologist William C. Young explains the reaction of a friend in Cairo to his suggestion that belly dancing might be an art form: *"One of the women present laughed and said 'But everyone knows how to do it. It doesn't take any special training; we learn from our mothers...so it's not an art' "* (37).

Because many Middle Easterners also dance to express tribal and community connections and to communicate with the spirit world, belly dancing must be placed within a cultural context in which dance is not mere entertainment. Mevlevi Sufis dance to enter into ecstatic trance states (Schimmel 179). Moroccan Zar and Tunisian Stambali dances are used for healing and to appease evil spirits (Somer 580). The Moroccan Guedra dancer confers blessings on her audience (Varga Dinicu, <u>Community Identity</u> 55).

Despite the fact that both women and men use dance in various ways, dance sometimes takes on additional significance as one of several distinctive spiritual practices that help to ameliorate women's narrowly defined roles and limited political status within Middle Eastern culture. As Lois Beck writes, "lacking full-status economic and political roles in the society at large, many women, often with unconscious intent, struggle for control and power through a 'manipulation of the supernatural' " (50-52). Although they challenge the doctrines of female submissiveness and seclusion, these rituals--including dance--that afford women a degree of spiritual power have been practiced alongside Islam for centuries. Dances that offer affirmations of feminine autonomy and spirituality have long endured--not always in spite of, but sometimes because of cultural conservatism.

Mothers teach their daughters to belly dance at or before puberty in order to strengthen the muscles they will need for pregnancy, childbirth, and nursing. An article in the <u>Australian Nursing Journal</u> asserts, "to the Middle Easterners, the idea of a woman going into childbirth without these 'exercises' would be like sending an athlete to the Olympics without any training" (Kananghinis). In some Moroccan Berber and Saudi Arabian communities, it was customary for a group of female friends and family members to dance alongside a woman as she danced her way through the pains of labor and childbirth (Varga Dinicu <u>Childbirth</u>). In her autobiography, the early Twentieth-century Armenian dancer Armen Ohanian speaks of this aspect of the belly dance, which she calls "one of our most sacred dances" (qtd. in Buonaventura 116).

> *It was our poem of the mystery and pain of motherhood...it represents maternity, the mysterious conception of life, the suffering and joy with which a new soul is brought into the world. . . . Such is our Asiatic veneration of motherhood, that there are countries and tribes whose most binding oath is sworn upon the stomach because it is from this sacred cup that humanity has issued.* (qtd. in Buonaventura 116)

However, even though belly dancing performs myriad social functions and nearly all Middle Eastern women learn the dance, female dancers and musicians who appear in front of men are--at best--regarded with ambivalence. To call an Egyptian man "the son of a dancer" is, according to van Nieuwkerk, a "serious term of abuse" (110).

Although Islamic culture was not the first to veil its women, veiling and seclusion have become central to contemporary fundamentalist Islamist doctrine. Thus, the dancer--an assertive, unveiled, unashamed woman in a public place--has become a potent political and cultural symbol. Since the 1980s, religious fundamentalism has forced many Egyptian belly dancers into retirement. Religious conservatives "occasionally disturb weddings, break the musician's instruments, and chase the female performers from the stage" (van Nieuwkerk 110). Dancers have become targets of police harassment and even assassination attempts (Brooks 216). Belly dancing has been banned from Egyptian television (van Nieuwkerk 65). Even among Cairo's historic clans of entertainers, very few families encourage their daughters to seek a career in dance (Brooks 220). Daniszewski explains, "During the past 20 years, the rise of political Islam in the Middle East has led to more puritanical attitudes on morality in general, creating a backlash against belly dance."

The status of belly dancing today follow women's social and political position--as it has throughout its history. Buonaventura writes, the belly dancer's "acceptability or unacceptability was intimately bound up with the role of women in society and with what was permitted and what was forbidden them" (11). As women's roles have changed, the dance has been sacred and secular, public and private, modern and traditional. Yet, through all these changes it has retained its fundamental nature as a very basic expression of camaraderie and joy. Buonaventura quotes a Tunisian dancer who says, *"In my countrycountry, everyone's a dancer.... A day I don't dance is a day I don't live"* (197).

GLOSSARY

'awâlim (singular: '<u>alma</u>): Female scholars or learned women who performed primarily for women in the harems. They wrote poetry, composed music, improvised, and sang. They also danced, but only for women.

Bedouin: Pastoralist, migrating tribes. Currently comprise approximately 1 percent of the population of the Middle East.

bint al-balad: Daughter of the country. Used in Egypt as a term for lower-middle class women who simultaneously display the traits of femininity and toughness.

burqa: Women's veil required under Taliban rule in Afghanistan. Loose-fitting in order to cover the curves of the body. Covers the face and hair. Wearer can only see out of a small embroidered netting in front of the eyes and nose.

cengi: Turkish female dancer.

chador: white fabric covering that conceals a woman's head and chest--required after puberty.

fatwa: Religious decree

fitna: Chaos, sexual disorder, beautiful woman.

ghawazee or (singular: <u>ghazîya</u>).: Primarily dancers who performed in the streets and in front of coffeehouses. They principally performed at saint's day celebrations and migrated from one mûlid festival to another. Some ghawâzî also sang.

hammam:. Sex-segregated public bath.

haram, harem: unlawful, protected, forbidden, woman, wife.

jahiliyya: The "time of ignorance" before Islam.

mûlid (Plural: mawâlid): Saint's day celebration.

odalisque: female slave.

Ouled Nail. Algerian women dancer/ occasional prostitutes who danced for their dowries. The tradition continued until the early twentieth century.

mujahideen: Holy warriors.

raks al-baladi: Dance of the people.

raks al-hawanem: Dance of the ladies.

raks al-sharqi: Dance of the East. Hybrid form of women's dance found throughout North Africa and the Middle East.

schikhatt: Moroccan women's dance performed for entertainment or at pre-wedding festivities, usually among women. Moroccan female dancer or troupe who performs the dance.

sheikha: wise woman.

zaffa: Wedding procession.

zaffat al-'arusa: The procession of the bride.

zhagareet: High-pitched " ya-la-la-la-la-la- la-la-laeeee" cry of encouragement or approval made by women.

zina: Forbidden sexual relationship. Any sexual relationship outside of marriage or concubinage. Homosexuality, fornication, adultery, etc.

CHAPTER 2

DEFINING THE BELLY DANCE

Any thorough investigation of another culture's art form must include concomitant research into its social, philosophical, historical, and religious context as well as an acknowledgment of the researcher's own artistic and cultural prejudices. In this light, a comparison between belly dancing in professional performance and ballet--which Edward Said calls "its Western equivalent as an art form" ("Farewell to Tahia" 230)--can accomplish two things. First, because many Westerners unconsciously evaluate most dances vis-à-vis ballet--the aesthetic foundation of most of our dance forms--this comparison can facilitate an understanding of why we tend to devaluate belly dancing as an art. Second, it removes belly dance from the realm of Orientalism and fantasy and restores it to its rightful place in dance history.

Many Americans have come to erroneous conclusions regarding belly dancing based upon versions they have seen in cartoons, movies, paintings, or ballet productions. Yet--because authentic belly dance makes its appearance primarily at non-mainstream venues such as ethnic restaurants, foreign films, and international festivals--most of these conclusions are based upon hybridizations that bear little resemblance to the traditional dance form. Even when belly dancing is presented by skilled professionals, it is often filtered through sexist and Orientalist biases and, consequently, misinterpreted or trivialized. One example is a 2002 _Denver Post_ article about a parade led by belly dancers. It carried the condescending headline, "Belly dancers

Jiggle in Holiday Season" (Will).

    This response is certainly not a new development. The short movie featuring a belly dancer called <u>Fatima's Dance</u>, filmed around 1896, was one of the first motion pictures ever censored (Buonaventura 105). American dancer Ted Shawn, who visited the Middle East in the early twentieth century, described the "unabashed animality" of Algerian Ouled Nail dancers (qtd. in Buonaventura 95). He said, "It is not a suggestive dance, for the simple reason that it leaves nothing to the imagination" (qtd. in Buonaventura 95). After they saw Middle Eastern female dancers at Chicago's 1893 World's Columbian Exposition, a group of dancing masters wrote a letter to the <u>Chicago Tribune</u> that called the performances depraved and immoral. They questioned whether "a thing decreed to be too vicious to be allowed to live in Spain in the eleventh century is good enough to for an exhibition in America's Fair and in this nineteenth century" (Carlton 46).

    Like these dancing masters, many Americans tend to look at art forms as evolutionary phenomena that reached their zenith in post-Renaissance Europe and the modern United States. As a result, they consider artistic styles from less-industrialized countries to be comparatively primitive and questionable as art. More questionable still--because they are assumed to be primarily sexual in nature--are women's dances (like hula, African, and belly dance) that highlight the pelvis. These dances' emphasizes upon a joyous corporeality is fundamentally different from Western art dance aesthetics.

    Belly dance and ballet have many other dissimilarities. The first is the use of the stage itself. Because it is performed on large stages, often by a large <u>corps de ballet</u>, ballet typically uses a lot of floor space and concentrates upon creating interesting and varied floor patterns. The stage and dancers are often raised above and physically separated from the audience. The dance is frequently choreographed. In contrast, belly dancers generally perform at ground level, sometimes surrounded by the audience--not a surprising custom given that that belly dancing is traditionally a social (rather than a performance) dance. Belly dance is most often performed, in both folk and stage forms, by a soloist. Before the 1920s, when Badia Masabni began to incorporate Western innovations into performances at her Casino Opera in Cairo, the dance was customarily improvised and performed "more or less on the spot" (Buonaventura 149), as American journalist G.W. Curtis describes in a performance given by Kutchuk Hanem in Esna, Egypt during the 1850s:

> *Suddenly the whole surface of her frame quivered in measure with the music. Her hands were raised, clapping the castanets, and she slowly turned upon herself, her right leg the pivot, marvellously convulsing all the muscles of her body. When she had completed the circuit of the spot on which she stood, she advanced slowly, all the muscles jerking in time to the music, and in solid, substantial spasms. It was a curious and wonderful gymnastic. There was no graceful dancing--only the movement of dancing when she advanced, throwing one leg before the other as gypsies dance. But the rest was most voluptuous motion . . . the soul of passion starting through every sense, and quivering in every limb....Suddenly stooping, still muscularly moving, Kutchuk fell upon her knees and writhed, with body, arms and head upon the*

floor, still in measure--still clanking the castanets, and arose in the same manner....she retreated, until the constantly downslipping (sic) shawl seemed only just clinging to her hips and making the same circuit upon herself, she sat down. (88)

This description also highlights another difference between the dance styles--the use of the arms and legs. In the same way that Western audiences do today, Curtis implicitly contrasts European dances--which emphasize stepping and the use of the limbs, rather than the use of the muscles--to Hanem's voluptuous motion, spasms, jerking, quivering, and convulsing. In his opinion, her "curious and wonderful gymnastic" is true dancing only when she steps forward, "as the Gypsies dance."

The bulk of ballet technique is comprised of gracefully positioning the limbs and body as they move through space. The earliest lessons for a beginning ballerina are posture, carriage, and alignment; next, the student learns the first through fifth positions of the arms and legs--all of which rotate around a nearly immobile torso. The legs turn dramatically outward in the hip sockets and are frequently separated or bent. They provide momentum, power, and grace to leaps and spins. The arms are often lifted over the head--either singly or together. The graceful extension of the arms, hands, legs, and feet visually elongate the body and draw attention away from the pelvis and torso.

The belly dance, in contrast, seldom uses leg kicks or extensions. The legs are customarily kept close together--even during traveling steps--and do not rotate outward dramatically (See Appendix, "Anisa's feet"). The knees continually flex and straighten in order to initiate pelvic movements. Most belly dancers perform barefoot with their feet flat on the floor. Their arms are regularly held below shoulder level, framing and calling attention to the torso and hips (See Appendix, "Rooshana").

Ballet and belly dance also have dramatically different definitions of the ideal female body. The female ballerina's great strength is channeled into an illusion of ethereal weightlessness. Her body is slim, supple, and youthful with small breasts and boyish contours. Quite the opposite, the ideal belly dancer's body in the Middle East is defined in an entirely different way. It has soft, womanly curves and is not necessarily young. Buonaventura portrays one Moroccan dancer as "a galleon in full sail" (169) . Rodenbeck says Egypt's indigenous performers-- currently facing an influx of foreign-born dancers--describe them as "too skinny, not generous enough in the shoulders and hips. . . ." (19)

Author Geraldine Brooks learned ballet as a child and studied belly dancing during her six years in the Middle East as a foreign correspondent for <u>The Wall Street Journal</u>. She describes her childhood experience with adolescent ballerinas' dismay regarding their budding bodies:

> *With its stress on elongation and fluttering extremities, ballet denied womanliness, requiring adult dancers to retain the shape of prepubescent girls. By the time I was fourteen the studio where I did my classes was a miserable place, full of students who knew they'd never become ballerinas. Their bodies had betrayed them by becoming too tall, too round, too womanly.* (217)

When Brooks attended her first belly dance performance,

featuring Souhair Zaki, she was delighted to see a different idealized female body type on display:

> *I could see... the beauty of a woman's body that was neither young nor thin. Souhair Zaki was the most celebrated dancer in Cairo, but she hadn't seen thirty in a while. Flesh clung heavily to her hips. Her abdomen bulged like a ripe pear....The dance drew the eye to the hips and abdomen; the very center of the female body's womanliness.* (216-217)

This disparity in ideal physiques is closely related to the greatest dissimilarity between the dance forms--the use of the midsection of the body. In ballet the upper body is almost always upright and still. The torso and pelvis twist and turn only subtly--usually during turns or to reinforce the graceful extension of the arms and legs. The ballerina's skills are leaping, spinning, flexibility, rapid and graceful leg and arm motions, and balance. She is often dressed in a skin-tight leotard and skirt or pants that emphasize the lean, lifted line of her body. Her art form--which uses the body as its instrument--paradoxically denies the earthbound weightiness of the body itself.

Camille Paglia calls the Caucasian 'line' of the Western dancer's body "the Greek God Apollo's hard incised edge. . . . His outflung arm represents head and upper body rebelling against chthonian pelvicism" (<u>Sexual Personae</u> 105). Even when Western dancers imitate the East, they typically avoid using the pelvis, as Buonaventura explains in her description of the pseudo-Oriental dancers who appeared in early Hollywood films:

> *The public's taste for heroines may have shifted*

> *from the pure Victorian heroine to the femme fatale, but most Hollywood femmes fatales were wholesome, nubile young girls with rosebud lips. When they danced, even though their costumes may have been diaphanous, they did not do anything as unacceptable as thrust their pelvises.* (137)

The ballerinas who dutifully perform the Arabian dance in every Christmas season's requisite performances of <u>The Nutcracker</u> follow the same pattern today. Although their serpentine arm motions and bare-bellied costumes are vaguely Oriental, their pelvises remain firmly locked in place.
Unlike the ballerina, the belly dancer is not weightless, androgynous, prepubescent, or ethereal. She is the opposite--heavy, voluptuous, mature, and feminine. Her art celebrates what Paglia calls pelvicism as its fundamental technique.

The focus of the dance is an extensive vocabulary of torso and hip isolations. The shoulders shimmy, twist, and roll. The chest slides, rotates, circles, lifts, and drops. The hips slide, twist, lift, drop, circle, undulate, shimmy, and quiver; the belly rolls and flutters, expands and contracts. The belly itself can often become a focal point of the dance. (See Appendix) The belly dancer's skill is demonstrated through the precision, isolation, variety, sequencing, and combination of these various movements--as illustrated in Goudsouzian's description of the Egyptian dancer Lucy, which appeared in Cairo's <u>Al-Ahram Weekly</u>:

> *Lucy's style can be dubbed the Perrier of belly-dance. She is an acquired taste. She makes no effort to captivate the audience with eye contact or coquettish gestures. She simply gyrates to the beat--*

but such a precise gyration. . . . Barramching! Lucy's hips jolt to the right. Barramching, ching, ching! Lucy's hips jut-jut-jut to the left. Her expressionless face cracks a smile as the audience begins to appreciate her physical rendition of the music. . . . (Goudsouzian)

Belly dancing challenges the Western viewer's most basic assumptions about dance--the relationship of dance to corporeality, the definition of beauty, the potential for new physical vocabularies, content, and aesthetics. Because of this, it can inspire us to expand our awareness of dance's creative and expressive possibilities. This allows belly dancing to perform one of art's most valuable functions--that of inviting its viewers to see the world in a different way.

CHAPTER 3

WOMEN'S PRIVATE DANCES

Ayatollah Khomeini once said "There is no fun in Islam" (Goodwin 106). In the modern Middle East, this statement seems to apply for the most part to women. Under regimes like the Taliban (in which--for women--simple acts like laughing in public, allowing a wisp of hair to peek out from beneath a head scarf, dressing in clothing that allowed the shape of body to be discernable, wearing makeup or attention-getting shoes, or visiting a beauty shop were illegal) dancing becomes a gesture of rebellion, even a political statement. Sciolino describes a spur-of-the-moment dance performance she witnessed in an Iranian aerobics studio. Although the studio was permitted to teach "athletic exercise" to women because it is considered healthy, dancing was forbidden. Even so, Sciolino met an aerobics instructor named Ladan who offered to dance for her at the end of one of her classes.

> *Ladan was dressed in a low-cut belly shirt, tight red and white paisley pedal pushers, big gold hoop earrings, and athletic shoes. But the dance she chose was pure Persian. She turned down the lights and put on the sinuous music. She thrust out her small breasts, revealing her slightly rounded belly and her navel, threw back her head, and put her arms over her head. She parted her wide lips . . . then she moved, swaying and undulating her way around the room. She outlined all the curves of*

her body with her hands and beckoned the audience [of women from the aerobics class] to her. It was a moment of sheer sensuality like others I have been invited to see from time to time in Iran. Men can be wonderfuly erotic when they show their skills in traditional dances. . . . But for women there is an additional dimension of freedom. So much of a woman's body is covered in public, so much is forbidden and repressed, that when the veil falls, even for a moment, there is a heightened sense of excitement. The women whistled through their teeth and hooted at Ladan as if she were a male stripper. Then, when the music stopped, Ladan and the other women put on their head scarves and the coats they call <u>roupoush</u> (outerwear) and left their refuge for the public space of the street This is how the Islamic Republic survives... (95)

Womens' havens like this aerobics studio are certainly nothing new. Women's and men's spaces--even within the home--have traditionally been separate in the Middle East. The word <u>harem</u> was derived from the Arabic word <u>haram</u>, which means unlawful, protected, or forbidden; <u>harem</u> can also mean woman or wife (Croutier 17). Female entertainers have long been fixtures in private women's places such as the <u>hammam</u>--the gender-segregated public bath--where women would relax, gossip, and enjoy music and dance (Buonaventura 84). Lady Mary Wortley Montagu, who lived in Turkey as the wife of the British Ambassador from 1716 to 1718, calls the <u>hammam</u> "the women's coffee house". She describes a group of dancers she saw at a hammam in Adrianople:

> *Nothing could be more artful or more proper to raise certain ideas. The tunes so soft! The motions so languishing! Accompanied with pauses and dying eyes; half falling back and then recovering themselves in so artful a manner that, I am very positive, the coldest and most rigid prude on earth could not have looked upon them without thinking of something not to be spoken of.*
> (qtd. in Buonaventura 84)

Dancers and singers were also brought into Egyptian and Turkish harems as entertainers and teachers. According to Nashat and Tucker, the seclusion of upper-class women provided many work opportunities for women of the lower classes.

> *The society's gender segregation promoted women's activities: upper-class women, secluded in the harem, required the services of lower-class women as entertainers, peddlers, cosmetologists, and midwives, who provided not only services but crucial links to the outside world"* (79).

Female seclusion in many parts of the contemporary Middle East continues to foster the preservation of women's separate traditions today. Hardy Campbell says Saudi women's arts--unlike those in more westernized regions--flourish, in part, because gender segregation allows women "to practice their music and dance without compromising their reputations" (61). Saudi women dance and perform music within sex-segregated venues such as women's universities, secondary schools, and charity functions.

The most prominent women in Saudi society--including women from the royal family--attend these dance and music performances. Hardy Campbell says these women's presence effectively endorses the events.

> *These women's attendance in effect puts the royal seal of approval on them and protects them from criticism by conservatives. . . . These well-to-do women sponsor their own parties, where music is played and dances are performed. The wedding party tradition is thriving. And as long as these parties remain in the Saudi women's realm, they are acceptable.* (66)

Hardy Campbell describes folk traditions such as dance as a cultural "escape valve" that allows "the participants and audiences to express emotions, frivolity, a spirit of play, and sometimes total abandon, in a public forum acceptable even in the most religiously conservative societies of the Gulf" (57-58). Thus, the female dance endures--not as the antithesis of the Middle Eastern woman--but as an integral part of her life. It is within this private women's realm that belly dancing continues to perform what may well be its most ancient role--in childbirth preparation and births.

CHAPTER 4

BELLY DANCING AND CHILDBIRTH

Many researchers have proposed that belly dancing was first developed to condition the muscles used in pregnancy and childbirth and as a childbirth technique that minimizes labor and birthing pains. This connection is reinforced by the discovery of terra cotta statues and paintings on stone walls that depict pregnant women in dance-like postures from Egypt and India--some of which date back to 25,000 B.C. (Helland 128). Dance and childbirth were also linked to various Goddesses such as the Egyptian Goddess Hathor. Women called upon Isis to "ensure a safe and speedy delivery" (Hawass 87). A Middle Kingdom story describes how Isis, Meshinet, and Kunum disguised themselves as dancing girls and assisted at the birth of the triplets who became the first three kings of Dynasty five:

> *Ruddedet felt the pangs and her labor was difficult. Then said the Majesty of Re, Lord of Sakhebu, to Isis, Nepthys, Meshinet and Kunum: 'Please go, deliver Ruddedet of the three children who are in her womb, who will assume this beneficent office in this whole land...' These gods set out, having changed their appearance to dancing girls... When they reached the house of Rawoser . . . he said unto them: 'My ladies, look, it is the woman who is in pain: her labor is difficult.' They said: 'Let us see her. We understand childbirth.'* Isis placed herself before her, Nepthys behind her, Heket

> *hastened the birth.... The child slid into her arms.... They washed him, having cut his naval cord, and laid him on a pillow of cloth. The birth of two more babies is described in the same way.* (Hawass 87)

Varga Dinicu describes a tradition practiced in less-westernized areas of Saudi Arabia at least until the 1950s in which women would dance in concentric circles around a woman in labor in order to hypnotize her, reduce the pain of her contractions, and facilitate the birth (<u>Childbirth</u>). Helland reports that Saudi Arabian women "cry out in sympathetic laments with a woman in labor" (128). Varga Dinicu discusses the use of dance in a Moroccan Berber birth ritual that she witnessed in 1967:

> *A special tent had been erected at one end of the village...[The woman in labor] was dressed in a lighter kaftan and d'fina and was squatting over a hollow, sweating up a storm. The other women had formed a series of circles, three deep around her... All the women were singing softly and undulating their abdomens, then sharply pulling them in several times... They repeated the movements while slowly moving the circles clockwise.*
>
> *The [woman in labor] would get up and do the movements in place for a few minutes and then squat for a few minutes and bear down. She didn't seem particularly agitated or in any pain. The only sign of strain was the perspiration that soaked her hair and forehead. We stopped only for midday prayers.... We drank some mint tea that* she

> *poured for every one of us and continued dancing.*
>
> *Less than half an hour later, she gave a gasp and we heard a soft thud. She lifted her <u>kaftan</u> and there was a baby in the hollow. She held up her hand: it wasn't over yet. Approximately fifteen minutes later, another gasp and another soft thud. It was twin boys. They were cleaned with soft, white tufts of lamb's wool dipped in cool tea, but the umbilical cords weren't cut until the afterbirth had been delivered. Then the cords were cut with a silver knife and the afterbirth was buried in the hollow that had received the newborn babies...*
> (<u>Childbirth</u>)

There may be a spiritual element to encircling the laboring mother as well. According to Schimmel, "The encircling of a sacred object--or a person... means to partake of its magical power or to endow it with power" (179).

According to Varga Dinicu, the use of group dance alongside a laboring woman is dying out in some areas of the Middle East. Nevertheless, childbirth training that uses belly dance and belly dance-type movements is still widespread. Kananghinis' <u>Australian Nursing Journal</u> article explains that dances using the pelvic muscles, which "tone the muscles for pregnancy," are taught to young women in the Middle East, Pacific, Africa, Asia, and India at the onset of menstruation and maintained throughout life to keep the muscles in peak condition. The article lists the following physical benefits:

> *The lower body movements, such as 'hip circles,' 'hip swings,' 'hip lifts,' and 'figure eights' were*

> *developed to strengthen the thighs, lower back and abdomen, as well as exercising the pelvic floor muscles... During pregnancy, all these movements are utilised during the labour process, as well as working through the labour (sic) pains... The 'hip shimmy' was developed as a cardiovascular and strengthening exercise, as well as assisting the baby down the birth canal during labour (sic)... the 'belly roll'... is actually copying the natural movement of the woman's body during labour (sic). Women in the Middle East practice this movement at least five years prior to conception to ensure an optimum muscular level was reached. It also toned up the abdomen muscles after birth ... All the upper body exercises.. strengthen the thoracic region, middle and upper back as well as the abdomen. . . the rib cage slides/circles are used to make it comfortable for the mother as the baby moves and stretches during the last trimester.* (Kananghinis)

Belly dancing has also taken on a new form in the West, where many of its techniques were incorporated into so-called natural childbirth methods (Latif). As women re-enter the fields of obstetrics and gynecology, which have been dominated in Europe--and, consequently, in post-colonial America--by men since the late Middle Ages (Mitford), natural childbirth methods are becoming increasingly popular.

The natural childbirth methods popular in the United States, however, train the mother only after pregnancy. Women in the Middle East learn their natural childbirth method--belly dancing--at puberty. Because they use it throughout their lives, they gain strength, flexibility, endurance, and confidence in the power and efficacy of their own bodies. During labor, they use the dance for distraction, to facilitate deep breathing, to relieve uterine and muscular discomfort, and to help move the baby into position for delivery. The belly dance has been refined and adapted through many millennia for exactly this purpose and has helped to bring untold numbers of babies into the world. Modern women are fortunate to have access to this ancient technique that can help make pregnancy, childbirth, and labor--the greatest physical trials many will ever endure--safer, happier, and more comfortable experiences.

CHAPTER 5
BELLY DANCING, SEXUALITY, AND SHAME

In the Middle East, belly dancing is--apparently inexplicably--simultaneously ubiquitous and dishonorable. Even though professional dancers are considered essential to various joyous occasions--particularly weddings--many people believe that, for women, professional performance is shameful. Professional dancers are thought to be selling--not their artistry--but their honor (Young 37). Dancing in public is considered "so dangerous to personal and family reputation that 'honorable' women should not be permitted to dance in commercial contexts" (Young 38).

Based on her fieldwork with Egyptian dancers, Van Nieuwkerk has concluded that--although professional entertainment is not shameful for men--it is for women, particularly those who work in nightclubs. This shame derives from the fact that women in Muslim culture have traditionally been defined a priori as sexual beings (Mernissi, Beyond the Veil 41). Because belly dancing is most often a woman's dance and women are primarily sexual creatures, belly dancing is considered sexual as well. The shame associated with commercial dancing, however, is not--as Westerners typically assume--because belly dancing is sexual. Professional belly dancing is shameful because it is performed by women in public.

Islam, in general, regards sexuality--within the proper marital restrictions--in a positive light. It considers "a contented and harmoniously lived sexuality" a prerequisite for personal and societal harmony (Mernissi, Beyond the Veil 44). Rather than setting up a polarity between body and spirit (as Christianity has), Islam vilifies women as symbols of social and sexual chaos.

Mernissi writes, "What is attacked and debased is not sexuality but women, as the embodiment of destruction, the symbol of disorder. The woman is <u>fitna</u>, the epitome of the uncontrollable, a living representative of the dangers of sexuality and its rampant disruptive potential" (<u>Beyond the Veil</u> 44).

Female seclusion, which reduces the female predilection to cause <u>fitna</u> (social chaos, also a term for a beautiful woman), has been considered the ideal since at least the fourteenth century. Under the strictest interpretations of Islamic law, women are expected to remain within the confines of their own home for almost their entire lives. Schlain quotes an Egyptian jurist who wrote that "a woman should leave her house on three occasions only: when she is conducted to the house of her bridegroom, on the deaths of her parents, and when she goes to her grave" (288). At various times in Middle Eastern history, seclusion was carried to such an extent that men would not even speak a woman's name aloud. So that he would not bring shame upon his wives, husbands never spoke about them in public. When a father announced the birth of a newborn daughter, he would call her "a veiled one," "a hidden one," or "a little stranger" (Croutier 151).

Removing women from public discourse and public spaces ostensibly protects them from predatory men; it also protects men-- who are supposed to give their entire "emotional attachment" to Allah--from women's seductive charms (Mernissi, <u>Beyond the Veil</u> 114).

According to Mernissi, veiling is simply an extension of the principle of female seclusion. When a woman intrudes into male space--any space outside of her part of the home--veiling allows her to be "present in the men's world, but invisible" (Mernissi, <u>Beyond the Veil</u> 143). Social, sexual, religious, and familial stability--because they rely upon female seclusion and veiling--become the woman's burden. As a result, even though many Middle Eastern men wear western clothing that breaks Islamic rules, women in many places are still expected or required to wear some sort of <u>hijab</u> (correct clothing), which ranges from a simple head scarf to a full <u>chador</u> or <u>burqua</u>.

Ironically, although gender segregation and veiling were developed in order to desexualize male/female encounters, in practice they often work in the opposite way. Because interactions between the sexes are rare, segregation and veiling increase their sexual content (Mernissi, <u>Beyond the Veil</u> 140). Van Nieuwkerk writes that performers' work behavior is considered disreputable because it "does not accord with prevailing ideas on femininity and respectability" (154-155).

> *Female singers and dancers may be an outstanding symbol of <u>fitna</u>, since they work with their seductive bodies to earn money. They do not keep the rules as prescribed by the orthodox discourse. They are not invisible, secluded, and devoting all their attention to the needs of the husband, the children, and the home . . .they uncover themselves, wear revealing clothing, and exhibit their attractiveness as women to gain a living. (van Nieuwkerk 158)*

This explains the religious conservatives' vehement opposition to female performers; dancers' actions are judged from a sexual--rather than artistic--perspective. Merely by leaving homes, working women commit an acts of sexual aggression (Mernissi, <u>Beyond the Veil</u> 144). Worse, a dancer--like any woman who leaves home unveiled--is considered "nude" and "sexually irresistible" (Mernissi, <u>Beyond the Veil</u> 144). Van

Nieuwkerk writes, "entertainers...make use of ...the feminine power to ensnare men and to create *fitna*...even the toughest man, if he sees a scantily dressed woman moving in front of him, must succumb to her" (Van Nieuwkerk 154-155).

Although many performers vehemently argue that belly dancing is a dance of joy, not sexuality, it is generally perceived as such by audiences in both the East and West. Additionally, the belly dance is historically associated with sexual ritual. Sachs writes that belly dance and other female solo dances that were performed professionally by the late Neolithic period "frequently employ the motif of libido and exhibition" (216). Even Buonaventura--who is certainly one of the most stalwart defenders of belly dancing as an art form--speaks of cabaret dancing as a "bizarre and yet oddly compelling" amalgam of glitz and "sexual promise" (57).

This connection between belly dancing and sexuality--anathema to many Western belly dancers--is actually the primary and ancient source of its power. Dancers exploit what Paglia--in her discussion of femme fatale actresses--calls "the world-disordering impact of legendary women like Delilah, Salome, and Helen of Troy" (Sex, Art, and American Culture 15). Belly dancers--fitna in the East, or femmes fatales in the West--draw upon and celebrate what Paglia calls "woman's ancient and eternal control of the sexual realm" (Sex, Art, and American Culture 15).

According to Mernissi, belly dancing was first developed by the Semites, who danced and performed ritualistic sexual acts "in the lustful temples of Ishtar, the [Babylonian] goddess of love . . . to honor Ishtar and celebrate women's sovereign right to self-determination" (Scheherazade 70). Sexual rituals performed in the temple honored "the fertility and sexual power of the Goddess"

(Lerner 130) and secured her ongoing blessings. The priestesses who performed dance and ritualized sexual acts in the temples of fertility goddesses were revered and honored (Lerner 127). After the Islamic conquest, however, sexual religious ritual and other non-marital, non-concubinage sexual relationships--many of which had practiced matrilineal descent and/or female sexual self-determination--were declared <u>zina,</u> or illicit. Sexual religious ritual and the dances that celebrated the Goddess were no longer considered sacred.

Male control of the sexuality of the women under their control--wives, daughters, sisters, concubines, and slaves--became intimately tied up with men's personal, familial, and tribal honor. As male control replaced female sexual self-determination, female virginity became a familial economic asset (Lerner 134) and came to be considered essential at the time of marriage. A Bedouin woman told Abu-Lughod that defloration was "the most important moment in a girl's life" (<u>Writing Women's Worlds</u> 201-202). A Muslim bride who does not bleed sufficiently may be returned to her family in disgrace and killed by her own relatives in order to restore her familial and tribal honor. (Goodwin 219)

Just like wedding celebrations, defloration rites are sometimes accompanied by singing and dancing. Abu-Lughod describes the semi-public nature of a Bedouin bride's defloration (timed by stopwatch at two minutes--which the bride's female relatives thought was too slow).

The groom arrived in an automobile caravan, then joined the bride and a few female relatives and a neighbor behind a closed door. His friends waited outside the door; women and girls in an adjoining courtyard sang and danced. The groom deflowered the struggling bride with a gauze-wrapped finger as her aunts pinned her in place, the honorably bloodied cloth was displayed for all to see, the men fired their rifles into the air and rushed away with the groom, then the women joined the bride--who was "dazed and limp in the arms of a relative, singing and dancing with relief. The cloth with its red spot of blood, a faint mark, was waved above our heads. . . . How beautiful!" (Abu Lughod, <u>Writing Women's Worlds</u> 191). Abu-Lughod recorded one of the songs the women sang about the happy occasion and the bride, Selima's, proof of her virginity.

> *Bravo! She was excellent*
> *she who didn't force down her father's eyelashes...*
> *Look at her cloth, girls*
> *You'd say it was burst pomegranates*
> *Little Selima, blessings on your marriage*
> *You're lit up by the faces of your kin*
> *Little Selima, bless you for hiding it*
> *Your brother came back proud as a Pasha*
> *Go tell her father to be happy*
> *The girl's blood came down on her hennaed feet*
> *The cloak I covered you with*
> *May God shine on your face, you filled it with light*
> (<u>Writing Women's Worlds</u> 192)

Like this celebration, many other wedding customs include dance and music. Some traditions have been untouched by westernization; others have been modified in response to gender roles that have changed in many areas over the past century-- sometimes because of internal factors, other times as a result of foreign influences. In certain communities, women and men continue--as they always have--to celebrate weddings separately.

In other areas, even ones that are otherwise conservative in respect to female veiling and seclusion, women and men celebrate and dance together. In some places where women and men customarily danced for one another or with one another until a few decades ago, they now dance apart. In other regions that have legislated strict gender segregation, women and men still dance together--but only behind closed doors. Wedding celebrations are often dramatic occasions when the veils--in both a literal and a figurative sense--that separate the genders in Islamic society come down.

CHAPTER 6

WEDDING DANCE TRADITIONS

Dance performs a variety of functions in wedding rituals. Family members, wedding guests, and professional performers dance during pre-wedding and post-wedding festivities and as participants in the procession that transports the bride from her family's residence to the home she will share with her husband. Because of the significance of female virginity prior to marriage, some wedding dance customs underscore the bride's transition from virgin into wife. In many traditions, dance symbolically enacts conjugal sexuality and the social transformation of the bride and groom into members of one another's families.

Bouhdiba writes that music and dance are used to announce lawful Islamic marriage--as opposed to <u>zina</u> relationships. A legitimate marriage must be accompanied by feasting, singing, dancing, and shouts of joy.

> *What distinguishes the lawful from the unlawful, the Prophet was fond of saying, was the drum and shouts of the <u>nikah</u> [marriage]. The aim of the ritual of marriage was precisely to surround the sexual relationship with the maximum publicity. The function of <u>nikah</u> is not to remove taboos, but to make them known. Beyond all possible forms of sexual relationship, <u>nikah</u> sanctifies one of them.* (Bouhdiba 15)

Dancing breaks down the usual barriers between the sexes--at times quite dramatically. In some traditions women and men dance for each other or perform one another's dances, as Mason observed during a seven-day wedding rite at a Libyan oasis community in 1975.

In this ritual, the young men and women first spend a few days dancing their own and the other gender's dances. The female guests dance and sing in the bride's honor. The highlight of the ceremony occurs when, as the women watch through a window or peek through a door, the men sing songs about love and sex as they thrust their pelvises "in rapid, repeated motions while their arms extend outward from the sides of the body and then come together as the palms resoundingly clap." Next, a veiled woman--usually the groom's young virgin sister, cousin, or neighbor--is led by the groom's younger brother into the men's room, carrying a white baton.

> *She stands completely still for several minutes...Then she begins her dance, which is a rapidly repeated, highly abbreviated twist of the hips from side-to-side. Simultaneously she shuffles on her heels very slowly up and down the line of dancing and singing males. Her baton is held continuously between both hands high above her head, moving horizontally to the rhythm of her shuffle...To bring her dance to a close, she spins completely around in a brisk turn as the baton cuts the still air with a white streak...the dancer's signal that she wishes one of the men to sing to her...The male singer...takes on the appearance of uncontrollable emotion...he must place one hand on*

> *the side of his head while he leans his elbow on the next man's shoulder.... His free hand is placed over his eyes... With a warbling moan, he begins by singing one line, stopping abruptly, and placing his hand back over his eyes. He continues in this manner, starting and stopping several times, describing in intimate, poetic detail the female body. Many of the details fit the young dancer in front of him. It is then that she may feel insulted to the point of anger by the singer's abusive lyrics, striking him over the head with her baton. Following the song, she returns to the bridal party in the next room. The men pause, then start their song and dance once again, hoping to lure the girl--or a new dancer--back.* (qtd. in Hanna, <u>Dance, Sex, and Gender</u> 49-50).

Mason observes that the mens' singing and dancing simultaneously praise and insult the female dancer. She is supposed to be anonymous and, thus, representative of women in general--with her baton as a symbol of her virginity and her male kinsmen's protection. Mason believes this wedding dance tradition "affirms the sharp line of demarcation between men and women and the avowed inferiority of the latter" (qtd. in Hanna, <u>Dance, Sex, and Gender</u> 51). Hanna notes, although the young woman appears to be in control of the men's actions, her control is illusory:

> *. . . when the women's bridal party tolerates verbal taunting about the supposed female sexual appetite, they reinforce the male stereotype of the sexually*

> *uncontrollable woman. The wedding dance clearly represents female virtue and male honor in the confluence of symbol and act.* (Dance, Sex, and Gender 50-51)

In this tradition, the men's pelvic thrusting, the girl's twisting hips, and their interactions are incontrovertibly sexual in nature. Varga Dinicu describes a Moroccan Berber wedding dance tradition--the Schikhatt--that is also blatantly sexual. The bride's family hosts all-day women's parties for three to seven days prior to the signing of the wedding contract. They hire a sheikha--a woman with "carnal knowledge extensive enough to teach it to others"--and her a troupe of Shikhat (or Schikhatt) dancers as party entertainment. The sheikha sings "raucous impromptu verses" that poke fun at the bride's family and guests. Between verses, the troupe performs the Schikhatt dance. Varga Dinicu explains that the Schikhatt employs exaggerated movements of the hips, stomach, and breasts in "very definitely an erotic dance and the movements have to be visible in spite of the large, loose caftans and d'finas they wear" (Community Identity 62).

> *...the sheikha, herself, dances in front of the bride-to-be, singing verses about the pleasures of marital relations that await the bride after the ordeal of the wedding night, and the loss of her virginity. With the Schikhatt movements, she demonstrates how the bride will be expected to move in the wedding bed...Both before and more so after the sheikha's dance for the bride, all the women get up at one time or another to dance with the troupe and*

each other, until they are tired and ready to go home for the day. (Community Identity 62)

The Schikhatt dancers or the sheikah may also perform for the men's wedding parties. "They smoke, drink heavily, joke, talk boldly, and fondle male guests in a way that would be taboo for women in other contexts" (Maher 111). If the bride's family is too poor to hire professional Schikhatt, unmarried village women perform for the men. "Their matronly sisters cry 'Shame!' but receive them equally when they come back" (Hanna, Dance, Sex, and Gender 52). Even the mother of the bride may herself engage in "licentious dancing" (Hanna, Dance, Sex, and Gender 52).

Maher reports that the Schikhatt are huryin (free) women (111). They live alone or in groups, and are commonly referred to as "women who do not want men to tell them what to do" (Hanna, Dance, Sex, and Gender 51). They are unmarried--they have usually been repudiated or deserted by their former husbands. For the Schikhatt, "being a free woman is a profession" (Hanna, Dance, Sex, and Gender 51). If they marry, they will mot be allowed to perform in public for the duration of the marriage (Varga Dinicu, Community Identity 63).

Although Varga Dinicu adamantly points out in Community Identity that Schikhatt "has nothing to do with raqs sharki," (62) the two dance forms certainly bear several features in common. Schikhatt may be a precursor to or descendant of the belly dance or simply a distinct regional expression of the sexual aspect of the marriage bond. Dancers who perform at Egyptian weddings sometimes invite the bride and groom to put their hands on her belly and breasts while she rolls her belly and moves her breasts.

Van Nieuwkerk observes that this behavior--which would be considered outrageous in any other context--is considered "innocent merriment and fun" when it is performed at a wedding (129). Professional performers are not the only dancers at weddings, yet non-professionals who dance often feel the need to excuse their behavior by explaining that they were carried away by the music or by joy. Van Nieuwkerk quotes an Egyptian housewife, who says, "I love dancing, but I only dance at the weddings of people who are very dear to me. . . . I danced at the wedding of my brother. . . . The feeling of happiness inside me made me forget myself" (131).

Abu-Lughod discusses the role of non-professional dance and the tensions that arise between the genders as mores in the pre-wedding womens' festivities in a rural Bedouin community change:

> *The beat was strong, and the girls sang song after song...At the end of each song, other women ululated and the girls resumed their drumming and rhymes... Suddenly, laughing as she protested, a girl would be dragged into the middle to dance. A shawl would appear and someone would knot it around her hips. Of the [older] women in the outer ring, only one or two would take special notice--usually her mother, perhaps an aunt. To get the older women involved, it was necessary to inspire someone from their midst. Then, to wild shouts of encouragement and wide smiles, this older and more robust woman would begin a shimmy of the hips that no younger girl could imitate...*

(Writing Women's Worlds 175-176)

Fifteen years earlier, women in this community were encouraged to dance in front of young men at wedding festivities. They followed the bride as she was carried in a litter or on the back of a camel during the wedding processional that brought her to her new home. The women danced--fully veiled, with their waists wrapped in the same type of man's thick white cloak that was worn by the bride--while young men serenaded them with a distinctive type of love song. Both women and men exchanged these love songs, some which were quite salacious. At the time of Abu-Lughod's visit, however, women and men celebrated weddings separately.

At this wedding, the groom's father was concerned that the sound of the women's festivities would carry to the men's party, where outsiders were present. Towards evening, he approached the women and complained about their noisy celebration. The women protested against his interference because ". . . the same men who when younger had sung such songs to women had now become elders. Unlike their fathers, these men felt they had to keep the women quiet when outsiders were there" (Writing Women's Worlds 185). One old woman expressed her sadness that weddings, circumcisions, sheep-shearings, and other gatherings-- because they were no longer celebrated with music and dance--had lost their appeal:

> ...the things they did before you can't do any more. Nowadays, weddings are small, like a shrunken old man. People used to really celebrate, staying up all night, for days! But they have become like the Muslim Brothers now. (Writing Women's Worlds

183)

William C. Young writes about other changes in wedding dance traditions (39-40). At Cairene weddings until about the 1930s, the mothers of the bride and groom danced together as an expression of farah (joy). By dancing together, the mothers of the bride and groom symbolized their relationship as new in-laws. A professional dancer also performed. She was paid by tips that the wedding guests placed for her in a handkerchief on the bride's lap.

Young believes dance performed important symbolic functions at these gatherings. Dance *"was a form of ritual work, not merely entertainment....As ritual work, it was highly valued and was considered an essential part of the wedding"* (39-40). The professional dancer's tips--because they were placed in the bride's lap--represented fertility. By giving the dancer's tips to the bride, the women guests encouraged the bride to feel welcome in her new community. Since the dancer's performance was one of the gifts presented to the bride by the groom's family, it enhanced the connectedness of the two extended families (39). After the 1940s, however, gender segregation was practiced less strictly at Cairo weddings. Consequently--because men could now watch women's dances--the mothers of the bride and groom no longer danced. According to Young, at this point dance became a socially stigmatized commodity rather than a traditional ritualized expression of community (40).

One of the most detailed early descriptions of Egyptian wedding dance traditions can be found in E. W. Lane's Manners and Customs of the Modern Egyptians. He describes various versions of the zaffat al-'arusa (the procession of the bride), during which the bride is escorted to her new home. The <u>zaffat al-ʿarusa</u> tradition is still common in Egyptian weddings today (Kent and Franken 79). Although it has been modified to suit the symbolism and tastes of the modern era, it still retains many key characteristics.

Until the twentieth century, <u>zaffa</u> processionals typically occurred outdoors in the streets near the bride's or groom's home--this is still true in approximately half of Cairene weddings today. Different social classes practiced their own <u>zaffa</u> traditions. Most included numerous participants: musicians and singers followed by married female friends of the bride, young unmarried girls, and the bride (sometimes riding a donkey or camel) with two female friends under a canopy carried by four men. The last members of the procession were another group of drummers and musicians. Poor families would not hire entertainers; they sang themselves (Kent and Franken 72).

After the 1940s and 1950s, the groom sometimes joined the processional. At this time, a belly dancer--immediately preceding the bride and groom--was also added to the <u>zaffa</u>. The central sexual symbolism--the married women, the virgins, and the bride's transition from virgin into sexual woman--remained. As Kent and Franken point out, the belly dancer placed the bride "in even sharper relief" (73).

> *The contrast derives from the social values ordaining that a dancer is everything a good woman should not be: free, independent, earning her own living, openly friendly to men, even flirtatious and seductive, and available to men on her own terms. . . . A belly dancer beside a bride demonstrates the power for evil (sexual chaos)*

inherent in women, even as their control and maintenance by men is the bedrock of the social order. (Kent and Franken 73)

During the 1970s--because many people had begun to think of outdoor <u>zaffa</u> processionals as old-fashioned--upper and middle-class Cairene weddings moved to hotels, in which the <u>zaffa</u> traveled from the lobby into the ballroom where the banquet would take place.   During the 1960s, a group of twelve to twenty male dancers called a <u>firqat</u> <u>zaffa</u> (<u>zaffa</u> troupe) sometimes joined the processional.   The men led the <u>zaffa</u>, dancing in two parallel rows, followed by the belly dancer, bride, and groom.   The belly dancer was sometimes omitted from outdoor <u>firqat</u> <u>zaffa</u> because of "possible objections or even disruptions by conservative spectators" (Kent and Franken 74) or for financial reasons, since the female dancer's fee was ten times that of the entire male troupe (Kent and Franken 74).

Although the modern <u>zaffa</u> has changed in style and symbolism, it is still an important "public proclamation of the legal union and familial approval of a marriage" (Kent and Franken 71). The wedding <u>zaffa</u> has also become a component of Arab-American weddings.   Kent and Franken write, "The use of belly-dancers in Arab-American weddings crosses all lines of religion and ethnicity and has become a firm tradition in a new land" (74).

Sciolino begins <u>Persian Mirrors; The Elusive Face of Iran</u> with a description of an Iranian wedding at which she was surprised to see women and men dancing together and listening to music--illegal acts in Iran.   She describes the women's colorful, revealing outfits and their hairstyles--"lacquered, teased, curled, dyed, twisted, braided, and frosted" (2).   She also describes one young woman's dance:

> *A young woman in a tight red dress and lipstick to match whipped a long pink chiffon scarf from her head to reveal waist-length curls. But it was her shoulders and hips that captivated the crowd. The shoulders and hips didn't stop rotating as she pranced hard on a concrete patio that had become a dance floor some hours before. She thrust her head back and her bosom forward, waving her scarf in the air as she beckoned others to join her.... I couldn't quite figure out how she moved all those body parts in so many different directions at the same time. But all the rotating and thrusting and scarf-waving worked, and soon there were two dozen Kurdish men in balloon pants and waist-length jackets on the dance floor with her. They linked arms in a wide circle. Now it was their turn to sway and thrust and kick and prance for the crowd. It looked like a frenzied rendition of the <u>hora</u>.* (Sciolino 1)

Sciolino says some of Iran's most religious women--just like the women at this wedding--"adorn themselves with makeup and jewelry behind high walls, then cover themselves in black on the streets" (6). She remarks that, in the Iranian Republic, simple acts like wearing beautiful clothing and a fancy hairstyle or dancing at a wedding party have become dramatic "acts of vanity and defiance" for women (2).

Buonaventura describes another intriguing wedding ritual she saw at a Cairene wedding, where the professional belly dancer was brought into position for a photograph between the bride and groom--each of whom placed a hand on her bare belly (38). It seems probable that this ritual is derived from one in which the Goddess' priestess-dancer would be asked to bestow the blessing of fertility on a newly-married couple.

This sort of public defiance of cultural norms has long been one of the belly dancer's roles. As Buonaventura explains, dancers "took on a surrogate role, indulging in an activity their audience was denied and could enjoy only vicariously" (50).

> *Professional performers belonged to communities who often paid lip service to Islamic custom, while maintaining their old beliefs . . . flouting convention, the dancers became the principal public expression of sensual joy and beauty, and so they have remained. In many countries of the ancient East, dancers were thought to bring good fortune, for something of the old 'divine' power of temple dancers clung to them. They were considered to have an essential role in all public and private celebrations, for besides bringing good fortune, they animated the festivities.* (50)

Hanna explains that, in the Middle East, "heterosexual dancing [was] banned in an attempt to eradicate goddess worship and isolate a female's sexuality for one man" (<u>Dance, Sex, and Gender</u> 48).

Even so, at weddings the dance retains vestiges of its old symbolism. Belly dancing--which has long been associated with sexuality and fertility (Hanna, <u>Dance, Sex, and Gender</u> 48) and the Goddess--still brings people together at wedding rituals and celebrations. The conservatives' objections to belly dancing, at weddings and elsewhere, are dramatic--however inadvertent--testimonies to its power. Although--as a remnant of the <u>jahiliyya</u>--belly dancing is decried as an agent of <u>fitna</u>, its enduring popularity testifies to its deep-seated cultural importance. Even though it is under attack, female independence as embodied in the belly dance has not been destroyed in the Islamic world.

CHAPTER 7

PERFORMANCE DANCE BEFORE
THE TWENTIETH CENTURY

Dance is one of the most ephemeral of the arts; in societies with traditions of female seclusion, women's dancing is more ephemeral still. Because female entertainment was--and frequently still is--considered shameful in the Middle East, Tucker explains that the history of entertainers "remains veiled in obscurity" (150). Social stigma concerning dancing "militated against official recognition of these women [dancers and other female performers] in the court records or elsewhere" (Tucker 150).

Western authors, travelers, and artists--who, because of strict gender segregation, rarely encountered "respectable" women--often disseminated portrayals of women that were based upon fantasies or that originated in encounters with women--including dancers, singers, prostitutes, and other "public women" who did not represent cultural norms.

As a result, many accounts of belly dancing come to us from men like Gustave Flaubert. Edward Said writes that Flaubert was only one of many Europeans who traveled to the Middle East in search of sexual adventures "unobtainable in Europe" (190). He says, "Virtually no European writer who wrote on or traveled to the Orient in the period after 1800 exempted himself or herself from this quest" (<u>Orientalism</u> 190).

Even so, in spite of these diverse obstacles to historic inquiry, it is clear that dance in general and belly dancing in particular have a very long history in the Middle East. It is also clear that the contemporary antipathy towards dancers is a relatively recent phenomenon.

In many places and during many historical periods performers were held in high esteem. Dancers from Egypt's fourth Dynasty (2680-2560 BC) were rewarded with gold necklaces and fine jewels (Buonaventura 44). Dancers in Egypt's New Kingdom--most of whom appear to have been female--performed for celebrations and religious functions. Daughters of elite families were taught dance, singing, and instrumental music in order to prepare them for their adult roles in temple rituals (Hawass 94). Their costume was "only a short kilt [or] practically nothing at all except a girdle" (Hawass 111). In Persia, India, Egypt, and Turkey, dance troupes were retained as part of royal households (Buonaventura 46). Other performers who were not under the protection of wealthy patrons danced in the streets. They were paid with coins that was tossed at their feet--later incorporated into the dancers' dresses, bodices, head coverings, and hip scarves to render them portable and protect them from theft (Buonaventura 44).

Although Europeans and Americans have a tendency to assume that dances that emphasize the limbs and de-emphasizie the pelvis are the norm, an examination of world dances reveals that "pelvic" dances like the belly dance are actually quite common--both historically and today. Buonaventura has amassed an extensive collection of references to "pelvic" dances from various places in the ancient world:

> The Greek writer Pollux describes a number of "fertility dances based on pelvic rotation, swaying of the hips and an exaggerated shaking of the bottom...which he

characterized by their 'swaying rotation of the hips' " (Lillian B. Lawler, qtd. in Buonaventura 29)

Dancers in Cadiz performed during the first century AD "sinking down with quivering thighs to the floor." (Juvenal, qtd. in Buonaventura 11)

The second-century historian Pausanius speaks of the kordax dance--which involved a rotation of the hips--being performed by Greek priestesses. (Buonaventura 32)

Propertius (about 60 B.C.) mentions Syrian women who had been hired to perform at a banquet who "danced lascivious dances to the sound of flutes, and accompanied themselves with castanets." (Buonaventura 43)

Ovid describes dancers from Cadiz, a Phoenician colony before it came under the leadership of Rome. "Graceful her arms, moving in subtle measure; insinuating she sways her hips." (qtd. in Buonaventura 43)

Juvenal depicts dancers who "sink to the ground and quiver with applause . . . a stimulus for languid lovers, nettles to whip rich men to live." (qtd. in Buonaventura 43)

Martial records dancers who would "swing lascivious loins in practised writhings." (qtd. in Buonaventura 43)

A seventh-century A.D. Persian scholar described the most

important skill of a great dancer as "a marked agility in twirling and swaying of the hips." (Mas'udi qtd. in Buonaventura 11)

Perhaps the most powerful famous dancer ever was the Empress Theodora, who married the Emperor Justinian and "became the power behind the throne in the Byzantine Empire" (Buonaventura 50).

Croutier discusses the <u>chengi</u> dancers who performed in Turkish harems during the Ottoman Empire. These women typically danced for the Sultan in groups of twelve--dressed in low-necked muslin blouses, velvet vests, and full skirts. Particularly beautiful and talented slaves were trained to become concubines in the Seraglio, "learning to dance, recite poetry, play musical instruments, and master the erotic arts" (Croutier 32). One Venetian diplomat who observed Ottoman dancing said it could "liquefy marble" (Coco 45). Dancers, singers, and dwarves entertained the women of the Seraglio as they gave birth. When one of the Sultan's daughters married, the celebration--which included feasting, music, entertainment, fireworks, and dancing--often lasted for several weeks.

The three classes of female entertainers who performed in Egypt during the eighteenth, nineteenth, and early twentieth centuries were very well documented by Western writers and travelers. The performers were hired for wedding celebrations, during parties for seven-day-old babies and circumcisions, at <u>fantasias</u>, during <u>mûlid</u> festivals, at the women's <u>hammam</u> (bathhouse) and in the harems (van Nieuwkerk 23-25). The groups had different performance skills and venues as well as different levels of status within the community. Van Nieuwkerk explains the differences between them.

The first group (the higher-class 'awâlim, singular: 'alma,), whose name means "female scholar" performed mainly for women in the harems. They wrote poetry, composed music, improvised, and sang. They also danced, but only for women. (26) The second group (the common 'awâlim) sang and danced for poorer people in the working-class quarters. (27)

The last group (the ghawazee or ghawâzî, singular: ghazîya) were primarily dancers who performed in the streets and in front of coffeehouses. They principally performed at mûlid (saint's day) celebrations, and migrated from one festival to another. Although they were sometimes invited to perform inside private homes, they usually performed in front of the house or in the courtyard.

The higher-class 'awâlim "were highly esteemed for their art" (van Nieuwkerk 26). Because they did not break the rules of proper female behavior by appearing in front of men, they maintained respect and social position. According to one source, even the master of the house could not enter the harem when the 'awâlim performed. If men were present when an 'alma performed, she was kept out of sight behind a wooden latticework screen or placed on an elevation that protruded into the courtyard from which she could be heard, but not seen (van Nieuwkerk 26).

Englishwoman Lucy Duff Gordon traveled to Egypt between 1862 and 1869, hoping to lessen the severity of her tuberculosis symptoms. She never regained her health; she died in Cairo in 1869. Because most of the travelers who describe Egypt's dancers were men--many of whom had contact with only lower-class dancers or dancer-prostitutes--Duff Gordon's observations are particularly enlightening because she visited places that were <u>haram</u> to male travelers. She describes one of the best-known of the '<u>awâlim</u>: "Sakna...is fifty-five--an ugly face, I am told . . . but the figure of a leopard, all grace and beauty, and a splendid voice of its kind, harsh but thrilling...the finesse and grace of her whole *Wesen* [manner] were ravishing..." (Duff Gordon 46).

Although the 'awâlim did not traditionally appear in front of men, the French soldiers sometimes forced them to do so. Denon, a soldier in Napoleon's army, reports an instance in which a general and two hundred soldiers persuaded dancers to perform:

> *Two of them began dancing, while the others sang, with an accompaniment of castanets, in the shape of cymbals, and of the size of a crown piece. . . . At the commencement the dance was voluptuous; it soon after became lascivious, and expressed, in the grossest and most indecent way, the giddy transports of the passions.* (Denon 232-234)

Denon reports that the dancers were invited into the harems to teach young women "all that may render them agreeable to their future husbands" (234).

> *They give them lessons of dancing, singing, gracefulness, and, in general, of all voluptuous attainments...They are admitted to the festivals which the grandees give to those of their own rank; and when, from time to time, a husband wishes to entertain his harem in a particular manner, they are also sent for.* (234)

Duff Gordon only once reports a performance by an '<u>alma</u>.

However, she attended many performances given by ghawâzî. Duff Gordon was surprised to learn that the ghawâzî dancers were not considered at all disreputable. "If a dancing-girl repents, the most respectable man may and does marry her, and no one blames or laughs at him" (Duff Gordon 139-140). The first time she saw a ghazîya perform, Duff Gordon thought her dance was "queer and dull... contortions, more or less graceful, very wonderful as gymnastic feats and no more" (Duff Gordon 112). Yet, after she saw a dancer named Latefeh, she wrote; "it was revealed to me" (360). Shortly before her death in Cairo, Duff Gordon wrote in a letter one last time about the ghawâzî.

> *I never quite know whether it is now four thousand years ago, or even ten thousand, when I am in the dreamy intoxication of a real Egyptian fantasia; nothing is so antique as the Ghawazee--the real dancing girls. They are still subject to religious ecstacies (sic) of a very curious kind, no doubt inherited from the remotest antiquity...Now that I am too ill to write I feel sorry that I did not persist and write on the beliefs of Egypt. . . . I honestly believe that knowledge will die with me which few others possess. You must recollect that the learned know books, and I know men, and what is still more difficult, women.* (360)

The ghawâzî were "one of the most important tourist sights" in Egypt after the eighteenth century (van Nieuwkerk 21). They formed communities on the outskirts of all the major cities; between six and eight thousand lived outside of Cairo in 1817. They performed at celebrations such as weddings, celebrations, and mûlid festivals. Although they are typically described as a separate tribe of gypsies or wanderers, they were Egyptian-speaking Muslims (van Nieuwkerk 26-27). They used various props--including scarves, sticks, sabers, vases, and lighted candles on their heads.

Unlike Duff Gordon, van Nieuwkerk writes that--because they appeared unveiled, smoked, and drank--the ghawâzî were not considered respectable (27). There is a common misconception that the ghawâzî were also prostitutes. Yet, according to most early travelers, this was not the case at the beginning of the nineteenth century.

However, for several reasons, the status of female dancers dropped precipitously over the course of the century. The greatest factors in the lowering of performers' status came as a results of the French occupation and the dancers' subsequent banishment to southern Egypt--after which many were forced to combine dancing with prostitution.

Napoleon's expedition to Egypt 1798 occurred during a time in which the country was politically weak. The dancers and other public entertainers were under state control and were heavily taxed. After Napoleon's army entered Cairo, the ʻawâlim left the capital. Although they returned toward the end of the occupation, they refused to entertain the French soldiers (Buonaventura 60). The poorest of the female singers, dancers and prostitutes, however, saw the soldiers as a source of income.

The French and Egyptian authorities tried to keep the dancers, singers, and prostitutes--who were accused of spreading syphilis and plague (van Nieuwkerk 30) away from the army--both for their own protection and to protect the soldiers. Eventually, the ghawâzî caused such unrest among the soldiers that Napoleon's generals had four hundred of them decapitated and thrown into the Nile (Helland 130).

In 1801, the English and Ottoman armies forced the French to retreat. After Muhammad 'Alî took power in 1811, he increased taxes--which again forced the 'awâlim and ghawâzî to flee from Cairo (van Nieuwkerk 31). Once more, some of the women left the city and followed the armies--this time Ottoman and Mameluke. In addition to performing for soldiers, dancers and singers were increasingly employed on foreigner's boats or for parties given for foreign visitors by counsels and governors. Van Nieuwkerk reports that, by this time, "the 'awâlim were increasingly described as singers and dancers, the ghawâzî as dancers and prostitutes" (31). The religious authorities fiercely opposed the dancers' performances for outsiders. "The excessive European interest in female dancers, and the fact that Europeans monopolized the dancer's services, intensified the dissatisfaction of the 'ulama' (religious leaders) and caused a more general Egyptian protest" (van Nieuwkerk 32).

In June, 1834 Muhammad 'Alî issued an edict that banished dancers, singers, and other so-called public women from Cairo. This action was taken--not because the women or their dancing were considered immoral--but in order to ensure that "the eyes of the infidels" would not defile them (van Nieuwkerk 31). Because it lumped dancers, singers, prostitutes, and 'awâlim all together, this ban seemed to blur the formerly clear distinctions between skilled entertainers, less-skilled entertainers, and prostitutes (Tucker 152-153).

After the banishment, male performers in women's costume and make-up replaced female dancers at Cairo festivals, weddings, and processionals. These men--known as khawal or ginks--were often beautiful and graceful. Their dance and demeanor were so credible that they sometimes "caused confusion among the spectators" (van Niewkerk 33). Flaubert attended several performances by male dancers during his 1849 visit to Egypt and enjoyed their dances more than those of the women. He remarked that the female dancers--with the exception of Kuchuk Hanem--were "far less good than . . . the male dancer in Cairo" (Lane 115-116). Flaubert's comments reveal the wretched conditions into which many female performers fell after their banishment from Cairo. Flaubert's companion Joseph commented that "all beautiful women dance badly" (116). Flaubert wrote describes the women's dances as brutal (115) and terrifying (121). He said Kuchuk Hanem was "no more than a machine" (220).

Although the dancers and singers were allowed to return to Cairo around 1850, public singing and dancing were still officially prohibited. Even so, female entertainers could be hired for various occasions (van Nieuwkerk 37-39). They continued to perform at weddings, mûlid festivals, and at special events such as the 1869 opening of the Suez Canal. Yet the loss of their traditional roles and consequent lowering of their status had irreparably damaged their profession.

After the British military occupation in 1882, entertainment once again became the focus of governmental control. The mûlid festivals were reformed and restricted and cabarets were forbidden since they were not considered "conducive to moral behavior" (Van Nieuwkerk 37). Within a few decades, however, new entertainment settings opened up. This gave dancers more opportunities to perform, increased their earning potential, and--sometime--brought them fame, well into the middle of the twentieth century. Van Nieuwkerk calls the early years of the twentieth century "the heyday of the 'awâlim" (49).

CHAPTER 8
THE TWENTIETH CENTURY

Van Nieuwkerk writes that new opportunities opened up for both male and female performers at the beginning of the twentieth century at café-chantants. Dancing was also offered in hotels, gardens, theatres, operas, restaurants, and nightclubs. During the early twentieth century many dancers continued to perform at weddings and other festive occasions. The 'awâlim were once again called upon to perform in the houses of the pashas as well as for the upper, lower, and middle-classes--primarily in the Delta and Cairo. As city celebrations became less gender segregated during the 1940s, the 'awâlim vanished from urban weddings, although they continued to performed in rural areas until the 1960s, while ghawâzî and male entertainers performed in Southern Egypt.

At this time, the dance was first called belly dancing in Egypt (van Neiuwkerk 39). Other performers found steady work at nightclubs for Arab and European tourists and variety theatres for Egyptian audiences. The cabaret style evolved during the 1920s in the nightclubs of Cairo, Algiers, and Beirut (Buonaventura 148). Lebanese dancer Badiaa Masabni opened the first Egyptian cabaret in 1926 in Cairo. She was responsible for many belly dancing innovations including snakelike motions of the arms, the use of choreography, and the use of the veil as a prop (see Appendix: "Rooshana," "Amina," and "A Dancer's Eyes"). She introduced a 6:00 p.m. matinee for women only "which was packed out every evening" (Buonaventura 149).

Masabni appeared in her first movie in 1936. In the wake of the film's huge success, music and dance became increasingly standard elements in Arab films. The most popular singers and dancers of the time became the most popular movie stars. Between the years of 1935 and 1965, virtually every Arab film included music and dance (Franken 267). Tahia Carioca--another of the dancers at Masabni's cabaret--appeared in theatre, stage plays, and more than 120 films.

Although actress-dancers were popular characters, women's respectability was judged in their movie roles just as it was judged in real life. Dancers were seldom cast as "respectable" women. They inevitably lost their man at the end of the movie to a "nice" girl. (Franken 266) Farida Fahmy broke away from the role of the seductive belly dancer and became extremely popular during 1960s and 1970s as a result of two movies that were made about the Mahmoud Reda Troupe, with which she performed. She appeared in both films as a <u>bint al-balad</u> (daughter of the country)--a happy, modestly-dressed, sweet, respectable Egyptian girl. Franken calls her "the antithesis of the belly dancers that appeared in cabarets and films" (275).

Since the 1980s, there has been a religious backlash against many forms of entertainment that have come to be considered un-Islamic. Although old films that feature dancers are still allowed (van Nieuwkerk 65), belly dancing has been banned from Egyptian television. <u>Ramadan</u> musicals with dancing have been banned in some areas (Brooks 213).

Van Nieuwkerk quotes one religious leader who says all forms of female entertainment are <u>haram</u>, and all female entertainers will go to hell (121). As a result of these sorts of pressures, dozens of female dancers, singers, and actresses have retired over the past twenty years--often unexpectedly and at the height of their careers. The womens' retirements all followed a similar pattern. Each appeared on a popular television program with Egyptian televangelist Sheik Mohamed Sharawi, denounced their profession, put on a veil, and received the sheik's blessing. Some Egyptians believe religious conservatives have set up a special expense account with which the Sheik pays off performers who retire on his show (Brooks 214). Brooks retells a Cairene joke from the 1990s:

> *Who are the second-best paid women in Egypt? The belly-dancers, of course, because the Saudi tourists throw hundred-dollar bills beneath their feet when they dance. Who are the best paid? The dancers who've retired for Allah, of course, because the Saudi sheiks throw thousand-dollar bills into their bank accounts when they stop dancing.* (214)

Performers are also pressured in other ways. Shortly after dancer Farida Seif el Nasr returned to dancing following her well-publicized retirement, an unknown assailant "attempted to murder her with a volley of gunshots" (Brooks 216). Authorities refused to give another performer the papers she needed to make the Hajj pilgrimage unless she quit dancing (Brooks 216). In 1977, twelve of the fourteen nightclubs on Cairo's Pyramid street were set on fire by arsonists; in 1986, several other nightclubs were burned down (van Nieuwkerk 64). Some journalists have proposed that dancers who tour the Arab countries or perform in cabarets should be stripped of their Egyptian citizenship. (Idris and Mahfouz, qtd. in El Saadawi 86) Nawal El Saadawi, Egypt's leading feminist author, calls belly dancing "a form of sexual provocation" (81).

Dancing among mixed-gender groups was banned in Iran after the 1979 revolution--along with chess, music, alcohol, and prostitution. Iranian-born dancer and teacher Mohammed Khordadian, who fled to America after the revolution, returned home for the first time in 2002. He was arrested in Tehran and convicted of "corrupting the nation's youth through classes and performances he gave in the United States" (Slackman). He has been barred from teaching dance classes for life and ordered to remain in Iran for the next decade to keep him away from what the court called a "provocative environment that could lead him to repeat the offenses" (Slackman).

Although many dancers retired over the course of the 1980s, others have continued to build successful careers. Rodenbeck writes that the top Egyptian stars "are reputed to make up to $10,000 a night" (19). Even so, faced with growing religious conservatism, fewer Egyptian women seek careers in dance. According to the Egyptian Arts Authority, 5,000 professional belly dancers were registered in 1957; only 372 were registered in 2000 (Danisweski).

Many of Cairo's latest dancers were born outside of the country. Cairo's nightspots feature dancers of a dozen nationalities: "Lucy at the Parisiana, Katya at the Andalus, Suzy and Yasmina at the Versailles, Budshra at Casino al-Mau'ad . . . Russians, Americans, Lebanese, Germans, Tunisians, and even the occasional Israeli star" (Rodenbeck 20). One club manager says, *"Seven or eight years ago, the Arabs used to come here, sit with a bottle of whiskey in front of them and stay up all night watching a show....Now the younger generation of Arabs don't go to the nightclubs....They prefer to dance themselves in a disco... Even for posh weddings, the long-standing tradition of hiring a belly dancer is waning....Classy people today want to have only to have a deejay"* (Daniszewski).

One of the last authentic ghawâzî troupes, the Banat Mazin, continues to perform. The father of the sisters who make up the troupe says he was "lucky to have been blessed with so many beautiful daughters because they had provided him with a handsome living" (Buonaventura 51)--a telling statement in a culture that typically places much higher value on sons than daughters.

Ironically, as the belly dance has hit its nadir at home, it has become increasingly popular throughout the world. There are now "Middle Eastern" dancers in Japan, South America, the countries of the former Soviet Union, (Daniszewski) Finland, Austria, Italy, Norway, Sweden, Singapore, Germany, (Hamdy) France, England, North America, and Australia. Performers throughout the world have embraced this ancient dance and developed their own distinctive styles. California's 22nd annual Rakkasah Middle Eastern Dance festival in 2001 drew over 3000 spectators and several hundred performers from thirteen states and seven countries.

Belly dancing has become truly international, and belly dancers are still--for many people--considered an essential part of their own cultures as well as cultural icons for tourists and other visitors. Suhair Zaki danced at the weddings of the daughters of Gamal Abdel Nasser and Anwar Sadat and for Richard Nixon (Sami).

Many other Americans have also developed an appreciation for the dance. Henry Kissinger made it a point to see Najwa Fouad's show every time he visited Egypt and brought his wife Nancy to see her perform. After seeing Fouad dance, Jimmy Carter told her; "You are truly magnificent. Everything Kissinger said about you is true" (Sami).

Clifford proposes that--despite the fact that the Western appropriation of belly dance can be criticized as a form of cultural colonization--it can, alternatively, be interpreted as a expression of female rebellion. He notes that belly dancing was very popular during two periods when Americans redefined the ideal female form--the 1920s and 30s, and the 1960s and 70s.

> *Historically in the West, the private practice of belly dancing is connected to . . . freedom from cultural norms. . . . In the salons and private homes of the elite in the 1920s and 30s, the dance focused on the aesthetics of the veil and interpretative gesture. The dance was positioned as a fine and refined art, as well as a novelty and an amusement, and corresponded with celebrating liberation from the corseted torso. Belly dancing emerged again in the 1970s, in the wake of the critique of western culture and embrace of the East by the counter-culture movements of the 1960s.* (Clifford)

Just like women in the Middle East, western women continue their struggle to redefine themselves against cultural norms that focus upon rigidly anti-woman values. Clifford explains what he calls the "preferred historical narrative" through which many Western performers define the dance--one in which feminine spirituality once again plays an important role:

> *While the western belly dancer appears as an object in a matrix of sign systems which code her body as a re-presentation of the East, as erotic, as fetishized, dancers themselves articulate a distinctly*

> *non-performance dimension of the dance which is not always dependent on external codes...the preferred historical narrative [by which dancers explain the dance] is generally...one of pre-Islamic and pre-Christian traditions which venerated feminine sexuality, 'the goddess', or motherhood.* (Clifford)

These women, simply because they are dancers, differ from most Americans, for whom--unlike so much of the rest of human society--dance is no longer part of celebration, ritual, or religion. Images of dancers, dancing shamans, priestesses, and hunters appear in innumerable early archaeological sites: European caves (including Lascaux, Trois Freres, La Cueva del Civil, Marsoulas, Hornos de La Pena, and Altamira), the Natal Drakensberg mountains in the Republic of South Africa, and Australian Bushmen and African rock art--in which portrayals of dance are exceeded only by those of hunting (Hanna, To Dance is Human 51). As Sachs notes, throughout human culture dance has been a nearly universal activity. He begins World History of the Dance with "The dance is the mother of the arts . . . " (3).

> *It is not a sin, proscribed by the priest or at best merely accepted by him, but is rather a sacred act and priestly office; not a pastime.... but a very serious activity of the entire tribe. On no occasion...could the dance be dispensed with. Birth, circumcision, and the consecration of maidens, marriage and death, planting and harvest, the celebrations of chieftains, hunting, war, and feasts, the changes of the moon and sickness--*

> *for all of these the dance is needed....dance in its essence is simply life on a higher level.* (Sachs 4-5)

Although Americans dance occasionally in dating rituals or consume dance as spectators (in the same way we use the arts in general), dance plays a very minor role in our lives. Perhaps we should examine the anthropologically anomalous paucity of dance expression in our own culture in the light of Sachs' observations about the very few groups that he categorizes as "danceless peoples." He notes that, within these groups, "Social life, play, festival, and music are lacking, as well as a belief in and conception of higher powers" (Sachs 11). If, as Hanna writes, "to dance is human" (<u>To Dance is Human</u> 3), how much of our humanity have we lost because we--as a culture--do not dance?

CHAPTER 9

THE RAKS AL-HAWANEM

Hannah outlines myriad cultural functions that dancing performs in human society:

> Dance metaphorically enacts and communicates status transformations in rites of passage. (112)

> Dance articulates, creates, and recreates power relationships. (133)

> Dance . . . allows an individual to become . . . impulsive after the weariness of conformity . . . Convention dictates which postures, stance, carriage or gait we assume in this or that area of life. . . . Dance is perceived as an escape from this restraint. (Safier, qtd. in Hanna 69)

> Dance is . . . the medium through which an individual . . . takes on the role of mediator and becomes a conduit of extraordinary power. Dancing, the individual iconically conveys supernatural essence. (110)

> Dance encourages relaxation both in reality and in illusion. (Safier, qtd. in Hanna 69)

> Dance may often be a vehicle of self-assertion symbolically establishing identity as a counter to colonialism, [or] a dominating power. (142)

Several of these cultural functions can be observed in modern belly dancing expressions--the cabaret dance, zaffa processionals, wedding parties, childbirth rituals, women's private gatherings, mûlid festivals, and other celebrations. Yet--because traditions vary significantly from tribe to tribe, from city to city and country to country, and between rural and urban areas--this does not and cannot form a complete listing. The dance--just as it has for thousands of years--continues to evolve.

In contrast to prevailing American stereotypes, belly dancing is not an anachronism of the harems performed by young, seductive, scantily-clad women for men's enjoyment. The reality is quite the opposite; an overwhelming majority of Middle Eastern women dance for celebration, camaraderie, exercise, and to bring their babies into the world--far from the gaze of men. For these women, the dance is a simple, spontaneous, traditional expression of joy.

For other women--those who break cultural norms by performing in front of men--dancing is not so simple. Women who dance in public--whether out of rebellion, economic necessity, or because they belong to subgroups that place less rigorous restrictions on female behavior--break social norms that require women to be silent, immobile, and invisible. Dancers refuse to be invisible; therefore, they cannot be respectable.

Dancers embody *fitna*. This power for sexual chaos and social disorder--which all women possess--is particularly dangerous in performers who dress in revealing clothing and move their enticing bodies in front of men. Just as Islamic society attempts to keep all women under control by legislating their dress, mobility, and behavior, dancers' conduct is controlled through social pressure, legislation, and--sometimes--intimidation.

Over the past twenty years female performers have been chased from stages, denied the papers they need to make the hajj, shot, banned from television, and harassed by police. Many of the dancers whose businesses were based on Muhammad Ali Street have left the performers' traditional neighborhood. A craftsman explains; "They became tired of the police bothering them....The police treated them like prostitutes, always busting into their apartments to see if there were men there...The pressure is too much" (Brooks 220). However, even as it faces fierce opposition at home, over the past century belly dancing has spread throughout much of the world--and its popularity continues to grow.

As the dance traveled throughout North Africa and the Middle East, as European travelers journeyed to the Orient, and as Oriental dancers ventured into the West it acquired various names: raks al-baladi (dance of the people) and raks al-hawanem (dance of the ladies) in Egypt, raks al-sharqi (dance of the East) in hybrid forms found throughout North Africa and the Middle East, danza serpiente (snake dance) in Spain, and houri's dance, Moorish dance, Nautch dance, hoochie koochie, dance du ventre (dance of the belly), and belly dance in America--where it was first introduced at the 1893 Chicago World's Columbian Exposition.

Yet this dance, which has been known by so many names, is still above all the raks al-hawanem--the dance of the ladies-- ladies who, today, live around the world. From our Western mindset--with its long-established notion that body and sexuality are antithetical to mind and civilization--it is easy to view belly dancing as capitulation to rigidly patriarchal culture rather than a refutation of it. However, within its historical context, it is undeniable that this a dance--not of female submission--but of power. The conservatives' opposition to the dance is, however inadvertently, a tacit acknowledgment its deep-seated cultural importance.

As Mernissi writes, "The whole [Muslim social] system is based on the assumption that women are powerful and dangerous beings. All sexual institutions . . . can be perceived as a strategy for containing their power" (Beyond the Veil 19). Within a patriarchal, patrilineal, patrilocal, polygamous culture, belly dancing remains a distinctive force of female initiative and power. Mernissi notes that belly dancing is a touchstone for Arab women in an unpredictable world. "In an Arab world suffering from aggressive globalization, everything seems to be changing at vertiginous speed, except for women's stubborn need, regardless of age and social class, for a self- empowering dose of the trance-like belly dance" (Scheherazade 71).

WORKS CITED

Abu-Lughod, Lila. <u>Writing Women's Worlds; Bedouin Stories</u>. Berkeley: University of California, 1993.

Al-Rawi, Rosina-Fawzia. <u>Grandmother's Secrets: the Ancient Rituals and Healing Power of Belly Dancing</u>. Trans. Monique Arav. New York: Interlink, 1999.

Beck, Lois. "The Religious Lives of Muslim Women." <u>Women in Contemporary Muslim Societies</u>. ed. Jane I. Smith Cranbury, NJ. and London: Associated University Presses, 1980.

Brooks, Geraldine. <u>Nine Parts of Desire; The Hidden World of Islamic Women</u>. New York: Anchor Books, 1995.

Buonaventura, Wendy. <u>Serpent of the Nile; Women and Dance of the Arab World</u>. Brooklyn: Interlink, 1998.

Carlton, Donna. <u>Looking for Little Egypt</u>. Bloomington, Indiana: IDD Books, 1994.

Clifford, James. "Thinking through veils: Questions of culture, criticism and the body." <u>Theatre Research International</u>. online, Summer 1997.

Coco, Carla. <u>Secrets of the Harem</u>. New York and Paris: Vendome, 1997.

Denon, Vivant. <u>Travels in Upper and Lower Egypt, in Company with Several Divisions of the French Army During the Campaigns of General Bonaparte in that Country</u>. 1803. trans. Arthur Aikin New York: Arno Press, 1973.

Croutier, Alex Lytle. <u>Harem; The World Behind the Veil</u>. New York: Abbeville, 1989.

Curtis, G.W. <u>Nile Notes of a Howadji</u>. London: Vizetelly, 1852.

Daniszewski, John. "Tummy trouble in Cairo" Middle East Online www.middle-east-online.com. September, 2000.

Dils, Ann and Cooper, Ann, ed. Moving History/Dancing Cultures; A Dance History Reader. Albright Middletown, Conn, Wesleyan University 2001.

El Saadawi, Nawal. The Hidden Face of Eve. New York: St. Martin's Press, 1980.

Flaubert, Gustave. Flaubert in Egypt; A Sensibility on Tour. trans. and ed. Steegmuller, Francis. New York: Penguin, 1972.

Franken, Margorie "Farida Fahmy and the Dancer's Image in Egyptian Film" Zuhur 1998, 265-281.

Goodwin, Jan. Price of Honor; Muslim Women Lift the Veil of Silence on the Islamic World. New York: Penguin, 1994.

Gordon, David C. Women Of Algeria, an Essay on Change. Cambridge: Harvard University, 1968.

Goudsouzian, Tanya. "Sikidim, Sikidim" Al-Ahram Weekly. Cairo: Issue 489 July 6-12, 2000.

Hamdy, Rasha. "The Allure of the Belly-Dance" Middle East Times. online 14 July, 2000.

Hanna, Judith Lynne. To Dance is Human; A Theory of Nonverbal Communication. Chicago: University of Chicago Press, 1987.

Hanna, Judith Lynne. Dance, Sex, and Gender; Signs of Identity, Dominance, Defiance, and Desire. Chicago: University of Chicago Press, 1988)

Hardy Campbell, Kay. "Folk Music and Dance in the Arabian Gulf and Saudi Arabia" Zuhur, 1998. 57-69.

Helland, Shawna. "The belly dance: Ancient Ritual to Cabaret Performance." Dils and Allbright , 2001. 136-143.

Kader, Soha Abdel. Egyptian Women in Changing Society, 1899-1987. Boulder and London: Lynne Reinner, 1987.

Kananghinis, Alia. "Belly Dancing Makes Birth Better." Australian Nursing Journal. 9, Issue 2 Aug. 2001.

Kent, Carolee and Franken, Marjorie. "A Procession Through Time; The Zaffat al-'arusa in Three Views." Zuhur, 1998. 71-80.

Latif, Angie. "The Birth of belly dance" arabia.com. online January 19, 2001.

Lerner, Gerda. The Creation of Patriarchy. Oxford: Oxford University, 1987.

Logan, Harriet. Unveiled: Voices of Women in Afghanistan. New York: ReganBooks, 2002.

Mernissi, Fatima. Beyond the Veil; Male-Female Dynamics in Modern Muslim Society. revised edition Bloomington and Indianapolis: Indiana University, 1987.

Mernissi, Fatima. Scheherazade Goes West. New York: Washington Square Press, 2001.

Mernissi, Fatima. The Veil and the Male Elite; A Feminist Interpretation of Women's Rights in Islam. Cambridge: Perseus, 1987.

Miller, Judith. God Has Ninety-nine Names; Reporting from a Militant Middle East. New York: Simon and Schuster, 1996.

Mitford, Jessica. The American Way of Birth. London: Victor Gollancz, 1992.

Paglia, Camille. Sexual Personae; Art and Decadence From Nefertiti to Emily Dickenson. New York: Vintage 1991.

Paglia, Camille. Sex, Art, and American Culture; Essays. New York: Vintage Books, 1992.

Rodenbeck, Max. Cairo, The City Victorious. New York: Random House, 1999.

Sachs, Curt. World History of The Dance. trans. Bessie Schönberg (New York: Norton, 1965)

Said, Edward W. "Farewell to Tahia" Zuhur, 2001, 228-232.

Said, Edward W. Orientalism. New York: Vintage Books, 1979.

Sami, Soheir. "Nagwa Fouad: Hours of Glory." <u>Al-Ahram Weekly</u>. online Cairo: August 13-19, 1998.

Shlain, Leonard. <u>The Alphabet Versus the Goddess; The Conflict Between Word and Image</u>. New York: Penguin/ Compass, 1999.

Schimmel, Annemarie. <u>Mystical Dimensions of Islam</u>. Chapel Hill, N.C.: University of North Carolina, 1975.

Sciolino, Elaine. <u>Persian Mirrors; The Elusive Face of Iran</u>. New York: The Free Press, a division of Simon and Schuster, 2000.

Slackman, Michael. "Iranian Court Convicts Dancer" <u>The Denver Post</u>. July, 9, 2002.

Somer, Eli. "Stambali: Dissociative Possession and Trance in a Tunisian Healing Dance." <u>Transcultural Psychiatry</u>. Volume 37. December, 2000.

Tucker, Judith E. <u>Women in Nineteenth Century Egypt</u> Cambridge: Cambridge University, 1985

van Nieuwkerk, Karin. <u>'A Trade Like Any Other' Female Singers and Dancers in Egypt</u>. Austin: University of Texas Press, 1995.

Varga Dinicu, Carolina. "Dance as Community Identity Among Selected Berber Nations of Morocco." Paper presented at the Joint Conference of the Congress on Research in dance and The Society of Dance History Scholars. June 11-13, 1993. Richards. 52-64.

Varga Dinicu, Carolina. "'Belly dancing' and Childbirth." <u>Habibi</u>. Volume 15, No. 1, online, Winter 1996.

Will, Ed. "Belly dancers Jiggle in Holiday Season." <u>The Denver Post</u>. December 6, 2002 Section FF.

Young, William C. "Women's Performance in Ritual Context: Weddings Among the Rashayda of Sudan." Zuhur. 1998, 37-55.

Zuhur, Sherifa, ed. <u>Colors of Enchantment; Theatre, Dance, Music, and the Visual Arts of the Middle East</u>. New York and Cairo: The

American University in Cairo Press, 2001.

Zuhur, Sherifa, ed. <u>Images of Enchantment; Visual and Performing Arts in the Middle East</u>. Cairo and New York: American University in Cairo Press, 1998.

APPENDIX

DANCING THE VEILS AWAY

NOTES ON THE PHOTOGRAPHS

> *Female singers and dancers may be an outstanding symbol of fitna... They are not invisible, secluded, and devoting all their attention to the needs of the husband, the children, and the home.*
> Karin van Nieuwkerk

    Belly dancing arose in cultures where women are locked away night and day--not only to keep them safe from men, but to keep men safe from them, where women who dance in front of men are considered sexually irresistible, where dances define identities, celebrate life transitions, exorcise demons, and bring babies into the world. Yet Western popular culture watered down this rich tradition and turned it into vapid harem girls, hootchie kootchie dancers, insipid Nutcracker acts, and half-dressed figures in National Geographic. Edward Said writes that Western artists typically depict Oriental women as "creatures of a male power-fantasy. They express unlimited sensuality, they are more or less stupid, and above all they are willing" (Orientalism 207).

    The belly dancers I know defy these stereotypes. They are like other artists--committed to their craft. They are like other dancers--crafting a fusion of body, music, and the raw substance of human emotion. They are like other women--battling for independent identities within cultures that force them into dependency and powerlessness. My goal with these photographs is to do justice to these dancers and their ancient art.

    The veils that appear as the central symbol in this work never force the dancers into anonymity, as women's traditional veils do. Instead, they swoop and flutter through the air or frame the dancer's beauty--transformed from symbols of oppression into buoyant grace.   These dancers are in motion--not posed for display; they dance, not for an audience, but for their own delight. Many reflect the spiritual element of the dance and its origins in birthing and fertility rites. These women dance their spiritual and sensual force.

  This dance has survived through the centuries because it has been passed down--grandmother to granddaughter, aunt to niece, sister to sister, mother to daughter. As Rosina-Rawzia Al-Rawi writes, in <u>Grandmother's Secrets</u>, "belly dancing is a dance form in which femininity and spirituality become one. This may be the reason why it is so taboo" (58). The tiger in a cage never forgets that it is a tiger. Likewise, women who have been veiled and secluded under the traditions of <u>harem</u> and <u>hijab</u>--reared with the certainty that they are powerful and dangerous creatures--dance a timeless, beautiful, powerful, and dangerous dance.

I want to walk beside you
through life
And you!
Want to put a ring in my nose
To pull me along.
Intoxicated by love,
I want to love you
And you!
Want to be god
Making and breaking me.
I want to dance forever in
the courtyard of your heart.
And you!
Singing songs of my helplessness
On the tambourine of my needs,
Want me to dance like a puppet.
I want to become a perfume
And permeate your body
But you!
Want to hide me in your pocket.
I want to cry:
And you!
Want to make me laugh as
you flick your fingers.

--Atiya Dawood, Sindhi Poet, Pakistan (Goodwin, facing acknowledgements page)

Printed in Great Britain
by Amazon